"Malcolm Duncan's niteblessings are simply inspirational! Having witnessed their birth and benefited from Malcom's wisdom for a while now, I'm thrilled that many others will now also be inspired, challenged, comforted, and blessed by his thought-provoking daily prayers for the world!"

Cathy LeFeuvre, author, broadcaster, leader

"I have been constantly impressed that Malcolm hears the heartbeat of our loving heavenly Father, and then expertly weaves words of prayer, reflection, honesty, and heart-cry into these niteblessings. They capture our emotions (sometimes happy, sometimes sad), and in that special moment cause us once again to reflect on His faithfulness, steadfastness, grace, and love.

Perhaps I should not be surprised, but as I read each one it seems they arrive at just the right time and say just the right thing for that particular day or moment. I have often found myself forwarding a niteblessing to someone in need.

I recommend you read this book and allow God to speak to you, encourage you, refresh you, and recharge you as God blesses you through each niteblessing."

Martin Pearson, pastor, Stroud Christian Fellowship

"Over the past six months our family has been through both joy and suffering, sometimes in the same everyday moments. The niteblessing has been a compass that last thing at night keeps us set on the course that takes us closer to the heart of God's love, and a peace that passes all understanding."

Gill Beardmore, lay minister

"I remember first receiving Malcolm's niteblessings at the end of Spring Harvest evening celebrations and was delighted when he then started writing these on social media. They have been a source of comfort, strength, and healing for me, friends, and family.

It's great to now have a book with these blessings in. I look forward to sharing them in my ministry and will continue to use them in my devotions."

Rev Karen Hilsden, Methodist minister

Previous titles

Building a Better World: Faith at Work for Change in Society
(Bloomsbury Continuum, 2006)

Kingdom Come: The Local Church as a Catalyst for Change
(Monarch, 2007)

Risk-takers: The Life God Intends for You
(Monarch, 2013)

Spring Harvest 2014 Theme Guide:
Your Daily Guide to Exploring Unbelievable
(Elevation, 2014)

Unbelievable: Confident Faith in a Sceptical World
(Monarch, 2014)

40 Days with Jesus: An Invitation to Know Him Better
(Monarch, 2015)

I Want to Be a God Gazer: Yearning for Intimacy with the Saviour
(Monarch, 2015)

Fleeting Shadows: How Christ Transforms the Darkness
(CWR, 2015)

One for All: The Foundations
(Monarch, 2017)

One for All: The Implications
(Monarch, 2017)

#Niteblessings

Meditations for the end of the day

MALCOLM DUNCAN

LION

Published by
Lion Hudson Limited
Wilkinson House, Jordan Hill Business Park
Banbury Road, Oxford OX2 8DR, England
www.lionhudson.com

ISBN 978 0 7459 8060 7

First edition 2018

A catalogue record for this book is available from the British Library

Printed and bound in Serbia, September 2018, LH55

This book is dedicated to Julie Moody and her family, and to Elaine Duncan. I thank God for you.

It is also dedicated to the memories of those we have each loved and lost. Gone, but never forgotten.

Lastly, I dedicate these niteblessings to every person who, like me, needs a daily reminder of the hope, grace, and love that can be found in God.

Contents

What are Niteblessings?   8

January   10

February   22

March   32

April   44

May   54

June   66

July   78

August   90

September   104

October   118

November   134

December   148

What are Niteblessings?

For some time now I have been writing a simple blessing each day. I share it with those who are connected to me on social media via my public page on Facebook (RevMalcolmDuncan) and on Twitter (@malcolmjduncan). My friends, family, and those who journey with me through these social media avenues have often commented that they would like to see them in a little book that you could carry with you on holiday or leave by your bedside at night. Or maybe even leave on a coffee table in a waiting room. Perhaps even on that window ledge near the loo?

I have been deeply moved by how God has used these little blessings. I have regularly received messages from people all over the world. I am touched by stories of people who have come to faith, who have been strengthened at a time of trial, or who have been reminded of the beautiful grace of God and His promises. Thousands upon thousands of people read them, and I pray that they will be a blessing to you, or to someone you know and love.

I have thousands of them filed away, so who knows – this may be the first of several little books of this sort. I pray they will be used by God to bless you, to bless others, and to somehow – in a small way – build confidence in Almighty God. You can dip into them or use them on a daily basis. Whatever works for you.

This volume of *#Niteblessings* was written during my time as pastor of Gold Hill Baptist Church in Buckinghamshire. Some of the blessings were fashioned in the fabric of our life together as a community of Christ. I am deeply grateful for my time there and remember the community with great fondness. As I now serve the congregation of Dundonald Elim Church in Northern Ireland, I am equally humbled by the privilege of walking with you. May God continue to knit our hearts together in love and purpose.

Whether you are already a follower of Jesus or are just exploring who He is and what He does, I pray these little blessings will help you.

I'd love to hear your stories of how they have helped. Just drop me a line on Twitter or on Facebook.

Soli Deo Gloria

Malcolm Duncan
County Down
October 2018

January

1st January In the year ahead may God's grace be yours. May you know God's peace through every storm, His hope through every valley, and His joy through every sadness.

2nd January May God's grace enable you to see a future laced with hope, and may you be given the gift of faith to trust Him in all things.

3rd January May God give you a fresh sense of His grace and love toward you, reminding you that your righteousness flows from Him.

4th January May you know God's steadfast love in your life. May His constancy steady you; His mercy assure you; and His faithfulness cover you.

5th January May God enable you to find fruitfulness where you now see fallowness. May He enable you to open your heart to new hope and to new things.

✦

6th January May God give new faith to you for dreams you have held in your heart for a long time, reviving hope in the face of unanswered prayer.

✦

7th January May God birth new desire in you to seek Him; new passion for the Father, new love for the Son, and a new hunger for the Spirit.

✦

8th January May God rain down His many blessings on your life; may you see that you are clothed in Christ; may you carry His light everywhere.

9th January May God give you the ability to say yes to Him; may you be given grace to put Him first, and to seek Him above all others at all times.

10th January May the good news of who Christ is bring hope to your soul; may you be reminded that He has scattered the darkness, and that there is hope.

11th January May you know the power of the Saviour in your life; when you are troubled may He bring peace; when you are lost may He bring direction.

12th January May you never forget the power of Christ. He is God with us; He is the One who saves. He is your deliverer, your rescuer, your life.

13th January May you remember that God has stepped into history for you. He knows your challenges; He has walked your road; He understands.

14th January May the One who conquered death for you conquer the fear of death in you. May you face this enemy with an assurance of victory always.

✦

15th January May God bless you with a deeper encounter with the Saviour, a deeper assurance of His love, and a deeper hunger for His presence.

✦

16th January May Christ pour out a fresh measure of the Holy Spirit upon you; may His power strengthen you in your weakness and give you courage.

✦

17th January May Christ remind you that His power in you is greater than any other. May He lift tiredness from you through rest, and may He lift fear through faith.

18th January May God's ocean of mercy flood your soul; may the aroma of His grace reach the edges of your life; may joy become your crown.

19th January May God's hope burn so brightly in your heart that it will captivate your thinking, saturate your imagination, and transform your life.

20th January May the power of Christ minister peace into your deepest struggle, and may you be given the gift of simple, childlike faith.

21st January May God keep those you love in perfect peace; may He give you His assurance that He never gives up on them; may He shield them.

22nd January May God's rich kindness flow over your life and wash away despair, sadness, and loss; may His beauty captivate your imagination.

23rd January May the Lord of life pour His life into you; may the God of grace be gracious to you; may the Father of hope make you hopeful.

24th January At the stroke of midnight may God remind you that night passes and that joy comes in the morning. Tears are only for a season.

25th January May sleep bring with it restoration: physically to your weary body, spiritually to your soul, and psychologically to your mind. May the worries and cares of the day be replaced with the peace of God that passes understanding.

26th January May all that Christ has for you be your experienced reality; may you be given a fresh gift of faith and a new experience of joy.

27th January May God's life be your life; may you be shaped by Christ, rooted in truth, empowered by His Spirit, transformed by grace, and drawn by hope.

✦

28th January May you see yourself as God does: loved, accepted, forgiven, restored. May you know the joy and freedom that repentance brings.

✦

29th January May you sense God's presence with you tonight, hearing His love in the silence. May He chase away fear and hold those you love tightly to His heart.

✦

30th January May you know the joy of placing your burdens on Christ's shoulders; may you know the joy of friendship with the Father; may you know the joy of the Spirit's constant companionship.

31st January As you come to the end of the month, may your worries about tomorrow be lifted by the presence of Jesus; may your disappointment in yourself be outweighed by your knowledge of God's love for you; may you be given the gift of seeing tomorrow as a new day.

February

1st February May you remember that Christ still calms the storms. May He speak calm to the waves that are battering your life. You are loved.

✦

2nd February May God grant you to know that in your moment of greatest failure – in the wake of your most profound mistakes – you are loved.

✦

3rd February May the darkness of your night be illuminated by the bright, beautiful light of Christ. The morning will break. There is hope.

✦

4th February May you discover new strength and determination as you sleep. As you rest, may God's voice speak love and restoration over you.

5th February May you know a fresh joy of sins forgiven, a fresh excitement at God's plans, and a fresh passion for His glory in the world.

6th February May your family be held in the strong love of Christ. May He draw those who have wandered back to Himself, and may they know joy.

7th February May the presence of the Holy Spirit in your life bring a deep sense of the Father's love, fresh forgiveness, and a passion for truth.

8th February May the Lord hold you close to His heart tonight. May you know the utter acceptance of a Father who never walks away from you.

9th February May the Lord deal tenderly with you. May He gently prise your hands open, removing those things that will bring harm or pain.

10th February May you know that your deepest heartbreak is understood by God; that you are never, ever alone. May you know the gift of peace.

11th February May you know the safety of God's promised presence and the power of God's assurance that He finishes what He starts in us.

12th February May you know the restoring power of God's grace in your life tonight and the strength to carry on. May He wipe away tiredness.

13th February

Tonight may you know God's arms extended toward you and His heart open to you. May Christ's grace draw you to the Father.

14th February May You be surrounded by God's angels, strengthened by God's Spirit, and held secure in God's love. May nothing alarm or harm you.

15th February May God's nearness give you peace. Nothing will happen to you that is beyond His knowledge; you are never beyond His reach.

16th February May you be given courage tonight to step into a new season of life; may the insecurity of yesterday be overcome by new possibilities.

17th February May you discover that the well of God's love is bottomless, and may you drink from it and find fresh hope.

18th February May you know the tight hold of the Father's grip tonight. No matter how difficult today has been, tomorrow holds fresh hope.

19th February May the challenges of today and the uncertainties of tomorrow be dissolved by the constant whisper of the Holy Spirit. God wins.

20th February May you be given a new sense of purpose, acceptance, and meaning from God; may your sadness and pain be washed away by God's love.

21st February May grace sustain you; may your soul find rest in God; may you discover the wonderful reality of the life that flows from Him.

22nd February May the deep joy of God be your daily experience, and may you never be able to plumb the depths of His wonderful mercy.

23rd February May you know the delight of God! May the blessing of God, which makes life rich and adds no sorrow, deeply enrich your soul always.

✦

24th February May you know deeply the indestructible force of God's commitment to you. However dark your life feels, God carries you through.

✦

25th February Tonight may you be given fresh peace. As you rest in sleep may God cleanse your mind, renew your spirit, and refresh your body.

✦

26th February May Christ's mercy cover you; may the Spirit's nearness still your soul; may the Father's love chase away all fear and anxiety.

27th February May the powerful promises of God sustain you through every moment of your life, and may God's strength undergird you always.

28th February Tonight, may all cares and worries be lifted from you as you sleep. May you awaken refreshed and replenished by the Holy Spirit.

29th February May the light of Christ chase shadows away; may the Spirit guide you as you navigate your way through tomorrow; may joy be yours.

March

1st March May God remind you that your failure is not fatal. May He bathe you in a fresh experience of His grace and forgiveness tonight.

2nd March May God's love pour into your heart and life tonight; may an encounter with God's Spirit profoundly strengthen your soul.

3rd March May the greatness of God leave you with a new appreciation of the vastness of His power and the beauty of His grace toward you.

4th March May you hear the whisper of God, and may you remember that we can only hear a whisper from those who are close to us.

5th March May God wrap His arms of protective and nurturing love around you tonight. May He shelter you, soothe your soul, and bless you.

6th March May you be restored by God, remembering that He is your peace, the hand on the tiller of your day, and the captain of your soul.

7th March May Jesus shower you with His love, His grace, and His hope. May your heart be tender, your spirit open, and your life laid down.

8th March May you rest in the adoption of God tonight. He is your Father and you are loved, accepted, and welcomed into His family.

9th March May the comfort and care of God guard your soul, protect your heart from breaking, and strengthen your resolve to walk in His grace.

✦

10th March May God remind you that nothing is stronger than His love, no-one is closer than His Spirit, and nowhere is beyond His sight.

✦

11th March May God enable you to rest well. May the stresses and blessings, sorrows and joys, all be absorbed by God's comforting presence.

✦

12th March May God comfort you by lifting the worries and anxieties of today from you as you sleep and bestowing deep peace upon you.

13th March May God's grace and love cascade over you like a waterfall; refreshing, renewing, and strengthening you by His ever-present Spirit.

14th March May God grace you with His grace; may He endow you with fresh faith, succour you with strength, and embolden you with courage.

✦

15th March May God remind you that one day the pain of every heartbreak will be broken and the heaviness of every sorrow will be lifted.

✦

16th March May God guard you ferociously, hold you tenderly, and speak to you personally as you rest. May He restore your soul and your mind.

✦

17th March May God remind you that He is by your side. May you be restored as you rest. May your hopes be revived, your joy rooted in Him.

18th March May the God who crafts oceans craft depth and beauty in you; may you know His strength and peace when the storms rage around you.

19th March May the blessing of God flood your life, sweeping away disappointment and regret, and replacing them with contentment, joy, and peace.

20th March May God's strong arms protect you as you sleep. May He give you a deep sense of rest and sleep. May you know that He is close.

21st March May you know that you stand in grace through Christ, seeing yourself as He sees you, your heart open to His life-changing power.

22nd March May God comfort and console you; may He hold you in the sadness and fear you feel; may He give you hope.

23rd March May you be hushed by the humility of a Saviour who knelt and washed the feet of His disciples. Such love!

✦

24th March May you hear the cry of Christ afresh, "It is finished." May all sorrow, sin, and shame be far from you.

✦

25th March May you know the goodness of God: that you are free because Christ was bound; healed because he was torn. Grace!

✦

26th March May God remind you that waiting is only for a season, not forever. May death's separation be swallowed by resurrection hope.

27th March May darkness be scattered, gloom dispelled, and the fear of death removed from your heart by the gloriously alive Jesus Christ.

28th March May God encounter you where you are; barren wildernesses becoming places of revelation with you caught up in His plans.

29th March May you lean hard into God tonight. May you know that He catches you and carries you. May His grace pour over you!

30th March May God shine through the translucent scars in your life, revealing His beauty and love to you and through you.

31st March As darkness falls, God is there to sustain you through the night, to watch over you as you sleep, to restore your weary body, and to replenish you with hope and joy for tomorrow.

April

1st April May God restore you tonight, may He wipe away the tears of the day, and may He give you assurance that He is always with you.

✦

2nd April May heaven's songs fill your heart. May you know God's love, hope, and grace. May your heart be tuned to His.

✦

3rd April May courage be your anthem. May hope be in your heart. In your darkest moments may life be found.

✦

4th April May God's nearness comfort you tonight; may He stir dreams of what could be and deal gently with regrets of the past.

5th April May God-the-restorer breathe fresh life into your body, soul, and spirit; may you awaken refreshed, inspired, and encouraged.

✦

6th April May God lead you to hope. May your doubts and fears be broken moments through which the Spirit whispers: "God is near."

✦

7th April May you know that you matter to God, that you have a place in His family, and that your life matters to Him and to others.

✦

8th April May your disappointments be few, your joys be many, and your hope an overflowing well. May God sustain you by His grace and mercy.

9th April May the presence of God still your soul, His grace liberate you, His beauty captivate you, His promise sustain you.

✦

10th April May God show you the possibilities of tomorrow, giving courage and confidence to step into them by His grace.

✦

11th April May God remind you that His love for you sits at the heart of your self-understanding. You are loved by Him no matter what!

✦

12th April May God instil in you a deep resilience, giving you grace and strength to face anything knowing that He is always near.

13th April As new life appears in the seasons around us, may you be reminded that God works in seasons in your life. May you remember that winter does not last forever, and may you be given grace to see signs of new life and fresh hope all around you.

14th April May your strength be restored. Despite what you face, may fresh courage and confidence fill your soul, and passion your heart.

15th April May you know that darkness always gives way to light; dusk is only a promise of dawn. May God sustain you with glorious hope.

16th April May your eyes see beyond what is around you physically to what is eternally true. Sadness fades. God's love endures forever.

17th April May God enable you to strengthen yourself in Him, remembering His promises, walking in His presence, and seeking His purposes.

18th April May God Himself be enough for you. May nothing else satisfy your soul. May you know the inexpressible joy of His grace.

✦

19th April May you experience the comfort of the Father. As you do, may worries, fears, and regrets be dissolved by His all-pervading grace.

✦

20th April May God strengthen your back or lighten your load.

✦

21st April As one day yields its end to another's beginning, always remember that God is closer than your breath and stronger than anything.

22nd April May Embracing Christ enfold you in His love; Forgiving Christ cascade His grace over you; Resurrected Christ give you life.

✦

23rd April May you know the whisper of God in your soul so clearly that His voice dispels fear, birthing peace and bringing deep comfort.

✦

24th April May God bring freedom to every area of your life, liberating you from lies, breaking the power of sin in your life, and giving you hope.

✦

25th April May you be stilled with God's peace, shielded with God's strength, enveloped by God's presence, and revived by God's Spirit.

26th April May God give you a new passion for His Kingdom, and may you see beyond your challenges of today to the hope of His future.

27th April Praying Christ will enfold you with the Spirit's presence so the raging storms around you appear no more than a gentle breeze.

28th April God's love is immeasurable, His grace inexplicable, and His commitments unshakeable. May you know these incomprehensible truths.

29th April May the God of life bring comfort to those who face the sorrow of death; may the God of hope give grace to those who face despair.

30th April May you be given the gifts of hope and faith – hearing the music of tomorrow and having the courage to dance to that music today.

May

1st May May God whisper His name into your soul. May you hear Him deep in your spirit, His tender, strong voice bringing peace and hope.

✦

2nd May May the coracle of God's promises carry you over life's unexpected waves and the wind of His Spirit guide you to safe harbour.

✦

3rd May May the night sky remind you of the power of God. As you see the stars, may you be reminded that He placed them in space, and may you remember that the same God who made the stars knows you and is able to sustain you, just as He sustains them.

✦

4th May May you remember that God weaves the rags of our lives into beautiful tapestries of grace, blending joy and sorrow, light and shade.

5th May May tomorrow bring a fresh sense of courage, born not from optimism but from a deep-rooted confidence in God's faithfulness to you.

✦

6th May May the Holy Spirit renew and refresh you, reminding you that God sees your situation and your struggles, and will see you through.

✦

7th May Let joy be your anthem! Let hope be your song! Let darkness flee because light has dawned! May life bubble up in you every day.

✦

8th May May Christ craft hope in you, the Spirit sustain you in every way, and the Father fill your heart with a sense of His deep love.

9th May May God's rhythm of rest be the rhyme of your life; His peaceful pace be where you place your steps. May His presence be enough.

10th May God is not far away; may you know His closeness. God always understands; may you know His wisdom. God is love; may you know His care.

✦

11th May May your rest be deep, your peace be profound, and your sense of God's Spirit be stronger than any sense of darkness or fear.

✦

12th May May you remember that God's timing is never wrong and His rhythm is always right. He alone can make a symphony of our lives. May your life be tuned to His.

✦

13th May May God's blessing drench you and flow into the lives of others through you. May you be content in Him, knowing above all that you are loved.

14th May Whatever you are facing, remember that God is closer than you think, stronger than you can imagine, and more gracious than you can understand. May you be given the gift of knowing Him more deeply in your life.

✦

15th May At day's end, may God remove the strains and stresses from your soul. As dawn breaks, may you rise refreshed and renewed in God.

✦

16th May Praying that God's beauty captivates you; that His gift of a simple moment takes your breath away; and that His nearness leaves you speechless.

17th May Tonight may you know the power of God in every area of your life. May He hold your gaze even though the storms rage around you.

18th May May God's stillness still you; may God's closeness comfort you; may God's goodness assure you; may God Himself be enough for you. May this be true for you tonight and always.

19th May May the Father remind you of His presence in your pain. May Christ give you a sense of forgiveness in your failure, and may the Spirit give you hope for a new day.

20th May May you know the blessing of resting in the Father's arms tonight. As you sleep, He smiles as He gazes at you, and His strong arms hold you close.

21st May May you know the truth that God's work in you is often gradual, always steady and deep. Though it may be unseen and is sometimes unfelt, may you be blessed by remembering that God is changing you from one degree of glory to another.

✦

22nd May May God bless you with deep rest tonight that satisfies and sustains you. May He rebuild your inner world gently but strongly with hope.

✦

23rd May May you remember that darkness cannot alter reality, it only conceals it. Tonight, may God's continual presence be your greater reality.

✦

24th May As you rest in the Holy Spirit's embrace tonight, may God disentangle your jumbled thoughts, rejuvenate your weary body, and restore your soul.

25th May May you be held in the hand of the One who knows you fully and loves you unconditionally, and may your sorrow be soothed by His touch.

26th May May God grant you grace to see beyond the moment you face right now, giving you the gift of faith to know that He is faithful in the sunshine and in the storm.

✦

27th May May your zest for life find its source in the author of life; may your love for others flow from the lover of your soul.

✦

28th May God give you space to be still, renewed, and strengthened. May the Spirit give you room to be you, unashamed and unafraid.

✦

29th May May you know the freedom of sins forgiven, the joy of being justified by grace, and the rest that comes from peace with God.

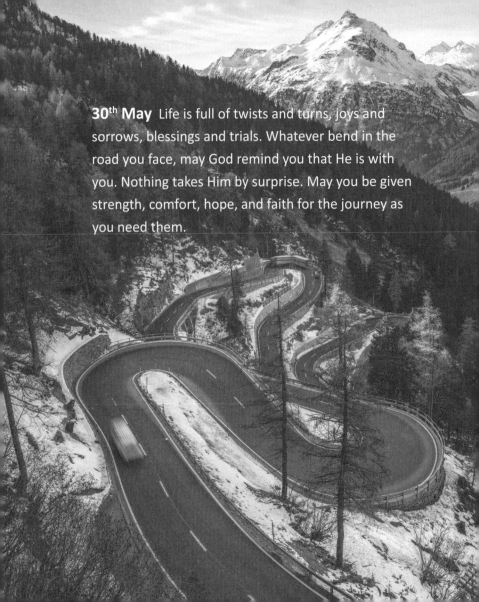

30th May Life is full of twists and turns, joys and sorrows, blessings and trials. Whatever bend in the road you face, may God remind you that He is with you. Nothing takes Him by surprise. May you be given strength, comfort, hope, and faith for the journey as you need them.

31st May May your restlessness be stilled by the Spirit's peace, and may you rise to face another day knowing that God makes all things new.

June

1st June May you be blessed with hope. When you reach the end of yourself, remember that God is always enough. May you rise with new strength.

2nd June May you know a hope that holds you, a love that lasts, and a peace that passes understanding; all found in the unchanging Jesus.

3rd June May you see possibility where others see powerlessness, and beauty where others see brokenness. May God lift your eyes to a new day.

4th June May God's love linger in your thoughts like freedom's fragrance, driving out despair, dispelling fear, and marking you with hope.

5th June As darkness falls, may God's grace light your way; as morning dawns, may Christ strengthen your soul; in all of your day may the Spirit give you fresh hope.

✦

6th June May you be given grace to hold things lightly and love people tightly. May you be freed from fear to walk in freedom.

✦

7th June May your deepest sorrow be comforted by the ever-present God. Nothing is stronger than His love, and no-one is closer than His Spirit. May comfort and peace flood your soul tonight and always.

✦

8th June May God give you peace in the depths of your soul, wisdom in the centre of your thinking, and courage at the heart of your will.

9th June May you be given grace to lay all you did today at Jesus' feet: successes, failures, achievements, and disappointments. May God remind you that He knows you inside out; that His love for you is deep enough to accept you and strong enough to hold you.

✦

10th June Amid the voices demanding attention and the competing expectations of life, may God's voice be clearest and His peace your rest.

✦

11th June May your joy outweigh your sorrow, may God's peace push out restlessness, and may hope be deeper than despair. May you trust God's love above all.

✦

12th June May your heart be lightened by God's love, and your weariness washed away by the Spirit's strength. May tomorrow bring fresh vision and new resolve.

13th June May God's stillness settle on you like dew in the morning; may joy rise in your spirit like a morning lark lifted on the wind.

14th June May God Himself be enough for you; your life centred on the One who is the centre of all things. His love is fathomless and endless.

✦

15th June May your imagination be stretched by the incarnation. May the mystery of God becoming a human being push you beyond comprehension into worship.

✦

16th June As you approach the middle of the year, may you remember that Christ always has the last word and His word is grace, always grace. May you be reminded that He will finish what He has started in you.

✦

17th June May Christ comfort you with His care; may you know that His presence will never be taken from you; His hope is always there.

18th June May God's beauty become your obsession; may His splendour dazzle you and His nearness leave you speechless; may He be your joy.

19th June Remember that the darkness of fear and isolation was shattered by the coming of Jesus Christ. May you remember that God has come to us and that we have hope.

20th June May you remember that there is nothing that you ever need face alone. Because God came to us in Christ, we know He understands.

21st June May you be given a gift of thankfulness so that your gratitude for what you've had exceeds your sorrow for what you've lost.

22nd June May your life be centred on the purposes of God; may His will become your desire; and may His pleasure become your delight.

✦

23rd June May the love of Christ be the foundation of your life. May you remember that God has given you the gifts of life and forgiveness and hope. May you enjoy them every day.

✦

24th June May the wonder wow you. Your waiting may seem to go on and on, but may you remember that God has come to us, that God is with us, and that God will come again.

✦

25th June May nothing disturb you. In the midst of the most profound uncertainties may Christ be your anchor. He is always enough.

26th June Joy defeats sorrow! It's true! May you be given faith to believe that the Maker of all the universe came down to earth as a child for you. May this reality become your experience more deeply day by day, and may this truth bring you life.

27th June May God take the shards of your everyday life and fashion them into the most beautiful, intricate, and dazzling mosaic of hope.

28th June May you be given the gift of fresh faith in a profound way today so that you see God before you see the challenges around you.

✦

29th June May God's plan become the starting point for your imagination; may you know that He will bring peace to the earth and to you.

✦

30th June May you rest well, knowing that God is present with every breath. He knows everything you face and will never walk away from you. May your heart be softened by His steadfast love. Even when He is silent, He is there.

July

1st July May the God of new beginnings fashion a new sense of adventure in you; may the first rays of dawn bring with them assurances of hope and possibilities of new discovery for you. Remember that night always gives way to day.

✦

2nd July Whatever you are facing, however you are feeling, rest in the presence of God. He knows, He cares, and He is with you always.

✦

3rd July May the promises of God sustain you, the presence of God surround you, and the purpose of God give you courage and resolve.

✦

4th July May you be able to hear God's voice above the noise and be given the faith to do as He asks even if it doesn't make sense.

5th July May you remember that God is never taken by surprise. He is with you at every twist and turn in life. You are never alone.

✦

6th July May you be reminded that God is listening. He cares more than you will ever know and He is closer than you could ever hope.

✦

7th July May God's word be whispered to your soul; may you be strengthened by the reminder that He still sees you, He still speaks through His word, and that He cares for you.

✦

8th July Remember that shadows only prove the presence of light; the night is only a precursor to the morning. May you be reminded that God is your light and your hope!

9th July May the miracle of new birth in Christ plant the seed of hope in you. May you carry the life and joy of Christ in your heart always.

✦

10th July May the beauty and wonder of Jesus leave you speechless in worship and breathless in anticipation of all that God has promised.

✦

11th July May God reach into your heart in a moment of grace and transformation that shapes you in Christ and breathes life into your soul.

✦

12th July May your restlessness be stilled by peace and your fear be forced away by a simple gift of faith. May hope be your dawn chorus.

13th July May you be given grace to endure; your flickering faith shielded by Christ's nail-pierced hands. The One who knows and loves you fully will never walk away from you.

14th July May you learn to walk in the shadow of God's grace. May the power of Christ's love reach into the depth of your soul and give you hope. May the empty cross become the anchor of your hope.

15th July May Emmanuel remind you He is near; may the Messiah show you He is your rescuer; may the light of the world illuminate your path.

16th July May God spread His blanket of grace over you tonight, shielding you from storms, protecting you from cold, and giving you comfort.

17th July May you know the incarnation's roaring reality: God has come near. May you know its quiet hope: God is close enough to hear His whisper.

18th July May your longing be met by God's hope; may your grief be swallowed by God's comfort; may your pain be dissolved by God's love.

19ᵗʰ July May God's presence shine over you like a star in the night sky. Even in the darkest moments He is present and He is enough.

20th July May you recall that by coming to us God has changed the world forever, and may you see again that at the crucible of the cross Jesus carried sin's weight for all who believe. May you be given the gift of faith to believe that He did this for you.

21st July May you be given the gifts of hope and peace so that your spirit is tuned to the Spirit of God and His grace. May nothing be stronger in you than the anchor of this hope and the presence of this peace.

22nd July May you remember that because God has come to us in Christ, the way has been cleared for you to live in peace and joy. Tonight, may you experience this peace and joy in new ways, deep within your soul.

23rd July As shadows lengthen, darkness creeping over the earth, may you remember that the light of the world is with you. He never leaves.

24th July Be assured that God knows you inside and out. When our world feels upside down He gives us strength to stand right way up. May you have the grace to stand.

✦

25th July Take courage: there is nothing that you need face alone, no fear that is stronger than the presence of Christ, and no threat that has the power to dislodge Christ from the centre of your heart unless you let it. May God give you fresh faith and courage tonight.

✦

26th July May you be graced with gladness; may you be held in hopefulness; may you be shielded by God's Spirit tonight and always.

✦

27th July May the God of grace and life show you that He is the only source of true life and flourishing. May He surround you with grace.

28th July May God bring a sense of freshness and hope that saturates your soul. He is constantly faithful. May He bless you always and remind you of His presence.

✦

29th July May your rest be deep, your sleep peaceful, your burdens lifted, your hope restored, your passion renewed, and your joy abundant.

✦

30th July May your deepest fears be drowned in the ocean of God's love; may anxieties be lifted from your shoulders, and may you know peace.

✦

31st July Whatever today has held, it has passed. May God sink your regrets in His mercy and guard your hope with His angels. Remember that He casts your sins into the sea of His forgetfulness, holds your future in His hands, and carries you always.

August

1st August May God's intervention in the world remind you that He is never far from his people; may His nearness give you courage.

2nd August May God remind you that He is your strength when you feel weak and that when you come to the end of yourself He is still there.

3rd August May you be held by knowing that God is holding you; the cares and burdens of the day lifted from you lightly by His gentle touch.

4th August May weariness be lifted by the Spirit's life, and heaviness be lifted by Christ's light yoke. May tomorrow be your fresh start.

5th August May your heart be held safely in the hands of God; may you know the freedom that comes from knowing He loves you and that your sins are forgiven; may you be released from the grip of other people's expectations. His love accepts you and has power to transform you.

6th August May you be stilled by the stillness of the Spirit; like oil on troubled water may He calm your fears and silence your anxieties.

✦

7th August May God's presence overcome your sense of absence, His melody reorder your discordant notes, and His gaze catch your attention.

✦

8th August May you know that God sees beyond your fragility, reaching out a tender, nailed-scarred hand to you. His grace refashions you.

✦

9th August May God's blessing rest upon you and rise within you tonight; may your heart beat to the rhythm of His peace; may you see the world through His eyes; may His voice be the whisper in your soul that assures you all will be well, and rest be your reality.

10th August As midnight strikes and darkness wraps around you, remember you have nothing to fear from the night. May God hold you through the sleeping hours in the security of His embrace; may your restlessness be stilled and your disquiet be quieted. May sleep restore you.

11th August May you sense the closeness of God: in the quiet whisper of the wind, the space between your thoughts, the momentary glance of your eye, the sigh at the end of a breath, and the time between waking and sleeping. In all of these and more, He is there. He always is.

12th August May the Lord of life enliven you; may the shepherd of your soul protect you and lead you to still waters; may God the Father remind you that He delights in you, that you are accepted and forgiven, and that you have nothing to prove.

13th August May your heart be lightened by the love of God. As you rest this night may He strengthen you in Spirit, renew your resolve, and lift anxiety and fear from your mind. May you face tomorrow with a steady eye and an open heart.

14th August May you listen to God's whisper above the world's roar, so familiar with His voice that you can tune out the noise around you.

15th August At dawn when all is possible, in midday heat when pressure mounts, as night falls and endings come, may hopefulness hold you.

16th August May you be lifted by the Spirit's presence, strengthened by Christ's grace, and liberated by the Father's love.

✦

17th August May you know that your heart is held in Jesus' hands; scarred hands that speak of sacrifice; tender hands that show His love.

✦

18th August May God's Spirit sing a song within your soul; may His melody of grace be louder than the cacophony of care and fear within you.

✦

19th August May you know that the Father gazes upon you, knows your heart, sees your worries, and is present by His Spirit to give you grace.

20th August May you rest in the restfulness that grows from the reality of the Spirit's presence. The One who gives life is always there.

✦

21st August As one day gives way to another, so may darkness give way to light, sadness yield to joy, and despair surrender to hope in you.

✦

22nd August May you be given fresh joy, deeply rooted in the reality of the resurrection and not constricted by the circumstances of life.

✦

23rd August As you journey on, may Christ be birthed in you. May the cry of Mary, the mother of Jesus, become the prayer of your heart, "Let it be to me according to your will."

24th August May you
have friends who love you for
who you are, not what they want
you to be, and may you know the
freedom of being yourself.

25th August May you know the truth beyond all truths that you are loved by your creator and that His arms are open wide for you always.

✦

26th August May you sense a growing murmur of excitement in your spirit as you walk with God. May the future carry greater promise for you than the past. May a new beginning stir in your soul.

✦

27th August May the angels' message ring out in your soul, "peace on earth and goodwill to all people"; may you know the Saviour's presence, and may you be a carrier of grace and a harbinger of hope to those around you.

✦

28th August May the peace of God rest on you like a warm blanket, protecting you from the cold winds of anxiety and the frosts of fear.

29th August May you discover the ability to choose joy; not an emotion but a deliberate decision to trust that God is good, no matter what.

30th August Amid all your uncertainty, may you know the certainty and commitment of God's love shown so clearly in the life and the love of His Son.

31st August May you be given the blessings of imagination and possibility so that you can see beyond what you face now and into what could be.

September

1st September May you know God's comfort, be renewed by God's power, and be strengthened by Christ's victory.

✦

2nd September May hope hold you solid, peace surround you like a sentinel, love assure you of acceptance, and joy blossom in you like a flower.

✦

3rd September May you remember that God is greater: greater than sin, sorrow, and weariness; greater than everything. He is worth waiting for.

✦

4th September May God be the whisper of love in your heart that thunders above the roaring world, the growling devil, and the screaming self.

5th September May hope rise in your life like dawn. As you look to the Son, may you remember that darkness passes and that hope's rays pierce the night.

✦

6th September May God be your stillness amid the chaos; your peace amid the squall; your focal point amid the clamour.

✦

7th September May you discover grace afresh. No matter what has happened in your life, may the love of God shown through Jesus give hope and strength.

✦

8th September May God lift weariness from your body and replace it with energy and strength, giving you fresh courage for a new day.

9th September As your life unfolds around you, may the power of hope lift your spirit, strengthen your resolve, and renew your courage. Hope is stronger than fear.

✦

10th September May heaven's hope transform your life, and may you remember that mourning only lasts for a season, for joy comes in the morning.

✦

11th September Tonight may your weariness be lifted; may you remember that God's strength never runs out and that He carries you through everything.

✦

12th September May God remind you that He turns mourning into dancing, exchanging ashes for beauty and the spirit of despair for the oil of gladness. May this be your experience of Him today.

13th September Tonight, may you know that death does not have the last word. God is stronger than your deepest sorrow.

14th September Tonight, may God give you strength to face whatever lies ahead. May you have a deep sense of His presence in all you face.

15th September May you remember that at this very moment the Lord Jesus Christ Himself is making intercession for you by His presence in heaven. He sees you, loves you, and is for you. He is your representative and your hope.

16th September May God enfold you in grace; may you know the grip of His hand; may He give you gifts of rest for tonight and hope for tomorrow.

17th September May the Holy Spirit light your way, illuminating your step by God's powerful word and holding a bright candle of hope before you.

18th September May you know the gift of friendships that sustain you; may you find the joy that comes from being accepted for who you are.

19th September May you know the strength that comes from vulnerability; the freedom that comes from openness. God's grace is the deepest well.

20th September May you be given gifts of thankfulness so your regret for what might have been is dwarfed by your gratitude for what has been.

21st September May kingdom values shape you; may Christ be the role model around whom your life revolves and the only comparison that matters to you.

22nd September May circumstances not dictate the health of your heart; may the health of your heart determine your view of your circumstances.

23rd September May you find respect for others beyond superficiality and the ability to see God's image in those with whom you deeply disagree.

24th September May you remember that even when nations are in uproar and kingdoms are falling, the voice of the Lord melts fear and brings hope. In the fiercest struggle He is still enough.

25th September May you remember that presidents and politicians come and go, but God is constant amid all uncertainty and His word endures forever.

26th September May peace rise in your heart like a high tide washing away disquiet; may hope rise like a dawn, bathing all you are in its rays.

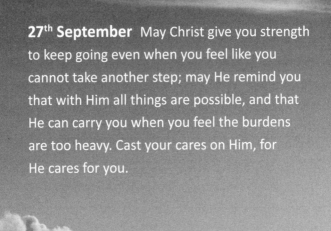

27th September May Christ give you strength to keep going even when you feel like you cannot take another step; may He remind you that with Him all things are possible, and that He can carry you when you feel the burdens are too heavy. Cast your cares on Him, for He cares for you.

28th September May your memory of failure be enveloped in the embrace of God's acceptance, and your defeats be swallowed by God's great victory.

29th September May you remember that the Spirit's whisper is louder than fear's roar; may knowing that God is near chase away despair's shadow.

30th September May courage take your hand if fear knocks at your door, and may faith fix your gaze on Jesus if uncertainty tries to catch your eye.

October

1ˢᵗ October May the God who holds the world in His hands remind you that He holds you too. As you face uncertainty, and as questions rise in your mind of what tomorrow might bring, may you be reminded that God is able to carry you and promises never to leave you.

2ⁿᵈ October May the God of the autumn enable you to let go of things that no longer matter; may the God of the winter strengthen you in the frost of sorrow; may the God of the spring help you to see new life being formed in you; may the God of summer cause an explosion of joy in your heart.

3rd October May you rest tonight knowing that God is there. He watches over you; He knows your deepest disappointment and your strongest longing. May He give you grace to trust Him to do a deep work as you sleep, straightening out your rough edges and giving you strength again.

4th October May God, who is rich in mercy, be merciful to you. May God, who is slow to anger, be patient and loving with you. May God, whose love is steadfast, be your constant hope. May God, who cannot ignore sin, remind you of the forgiveness wrought for you at the Cross. May you rest in the arms of almighty God this night and every night.

5th October As the world around you clamours for power, success, and position, may you be given grace to be content with what God is doing in your life, your family, and your desires. May you discover the great joy that comes from knowing that He is enough.

6th October May you fall in love with God all over again, captivated by His word, drawn by His Spirit, and embraced by His Son. May the Father surround you with a song of hope and life.

7th October May you be given the gift of seeing your life through God's eyes. May the obstacles you face become opportunities for growth. May the uncertainties you grapple with become moments in which you learn to trust God more deeply and follow Him more closely.

8th October May you find a new delight in God's word and its message of hope. May you read it with eyes of faith, noticing yourself in the story and seeing that God is our hero. May you be given a new sense of delight in the ways and purposes of God, and may weariness be lifted from your spiritual life.

9th October May the gift of God's presence still your soul. May the clamouring voices around you be hushed by the Spirit's nearness. May your hope come from God, who alone is the Maker of heaven and earth.

✦

10th October May you experience God in new ways today. May He release fresh gifts in your life and reveal new fruit of His Spirit's presence. May faith, hope, and love abound in you today.

✦

11th October As you leave the cares of today behind, may you be given grace not to pick them up again. Instead, may your heart be light, your soul at peace, and your mind stilled with the Spirit's promised presence.

12th October Life is sometimes hard, and we do not have all the answers. Amid the questions you might have tonight, may you hear the voice of God whispering to you, "I am all your answers. One day I will answer every question you have, and on that day the questions will no longer matter." May you be given the gift of faith.

13th October May you be reminded that God has never left you, and that He never will. Even when you have felt like He has not been there, He has always been by your side. May God show you again that He never breaks His promises – and He has promised never to leave you.

14th October May the joy of your God rise within you like high tide. May celebration and hope break upon you like the rising sun. May you know hope in new measure, and faith in new strength today.

15th October As the world rages around you, may you know that God is with you. May you hear Him whisper in your heart, "Well done, good and faithful servant." May He always have the first place in your heart.

16th October May you be liberated from fear and oppression. May God lift your eyes from those things that are distractions, and may He remind you of what really matters. May you be given the ability to let go of hurt and offence, and to embrace the mercy of God afresh.

✦

17th October God gives strength to the weary. He sets the lonely among families. He cares for the orphan and the widow. May you know His strength, the companionship of His people, and His love and care today.

✦

18th October As you wait for God to answer your prayer, may your heart be turned toward Him and your spirit be kept in step with the Spirit of life. May you learn the gift of obedience and be given the grace to trust.

19th October May your family know peace. May those you love be held securely in the love of God. May your prayers for them be answered, and may you be given a fresh gift of love for those who are closest to you.

20th **October** May you be given the gift of thankfulness today so that you can see the mercy and generosity of God all around you. May you see Him in the small things and in the big things. May your heart be lightened by the ability to be grateful.

✦

21st **October** May you learn the art of resting in God. May He remind you that you have nothing to prove with Him, and that His greatest delight is to spend time with you. May you enjoy the company of God and listen for His chuckle of delight over you.

✦

22nd **October** May you see others as God sees them and be given the ability to love them as He loves them. May you see beauty where others see ashes, and hope where others see despair. May your life display the mercy of God to others.

23rd October May your disappointments and regrets be swallowed by the lavish grace and promises of God. When you reach the end of yourself may you be reminded that He is always there to carry you. He is your strength and your song.

✦

24th October May you have a fresh vision of God – majestic in mercy, powerful in His promises, and faithful always. May He capture your imagination again today, inspiring you to live well, love deeply, and serve faithfully.

✦

25th October May tomorrow bring gifts of fresh courage, fresh hope, and fresh strength. May God remind you that sometimes you simply have to leave your regrets of the day at His feet. He can deal with them more graciously and effectively than you can.

26th October May the myriads of ways in which God has held you become evident to you in some way today. May you see His grace like a diamond, glinting in the light of the sun and reminding you that He cares for you.

27th October May you know the power of choice tonight, and may you be given grace to choose Christ and put Him first. Even if you do not feel like it, may you be given grace to do it.

28th October May the future God has for you inspire you to live well today. May you be reminded that He will complete His work in you.

29th October Our lives are intricate and delicate – and God is gracious and kind. Where you feel broken may He bring wholeness, where you feel weak may He bring strength, where you feel useless may He bring purpose. May you know He is on your side.

30th October May you be given grace to love deeply, to forgive quickly, and to serve unconditionally. May you be given the ability to accept yourself and to see how deeply God loves you, how quickly He forgives you and how unconditionally He stands by you.

31st October May the glorious, beautiful, breathtaking love of God shown to the world in Christ be shown to you afresh tonight. May you be left speechless at His mercy, and may you kneel before the creator of the world in thanks for His love for you.

November

1st November

May you hold on to the
reality that God holds on to
you. Remember that you were not
made for tears, and that one day they will
come to an end. May you share God's joy

2ⁿᵈ November May Christ's light illuminate the path before you, His forgiveness remove your regrets from the path behind, and His grace give you joy.

3rd November May you know God's melody of grace sung over your life and the symphony of His love for you playing in your soul eternally.

✦

4th November May God grant you simplicity of faith to know that He is good and it will all be okay in the end. If it is not okay, then it is not the end.

✦

5th November May God's compassion encompass you; may His wholeness make you whole; may His hope make you hopeful; and may His courage make you courageous.

✦

6th November As the flame of a fire blazes brightly in the night so may the fire of the Spirit blaze brightly in your heart, no matter what darkness may surround you.

7th November May the Spirit who brings truth to life bring life to you through the truth. May each breath you take remind you of God's constant presence.

8th November May God, who knows the end from the beginning, reach back into your present from your assured future and give you strength and hope.

9th November May you know that no matter what this day has held, tonight God is able to restore you, refresh you, and reignite your passion for Him.

10th November May God bless you so deeply that you sleep in peace, dream of new and brighter days, and awake strengthened in your resolve for Christ.

11th November May memories of those who have
gone before you bring you gratitude for their lives, and
may God use their example to give you determination
to live well and to stand for what is right.

✦

12th November Remember that God is good and
that His love endures forever. May you know this to
be true when you do not feel it, and may it shape you
when you do not see it.

✦

13th November May the sacred power of the Trinity
surround you tonight: the Father fashioning you, the
Son restoring you, and the Spirit transforming you.

✦

14th November May God's angels encamp around
you. May trust in God guard the chambers of your
heart. May hope drive out fear and despair.

15th November May the powerful promises of God sustain you when all seems to have fallen away. May His closeness chase away any shadows or fear.

16th November May peace be your portion and grace be your garland. May the gentle wind of the Spirit blow all fear far from your home and those you love.

✦

17th November May the weariness of the day be washed away by the rest the Father gives you this night. May He bridle your thoughts of tomorrow until dawn.

✦

18th November May you know the exhilaration of trying. May your fears of failure be swallowed by your longing for something new.

✦

19th November May God's nearness still you; may His gentleness soothe you; may His patience reassure you; may His assurance assuage your deepest insecurities.

20th November May you have a transformed understanding of yourself and your place in the world; may you know the deep joy of sins forgiven and the freedom of the Father's acceptance.

✦

21st November May your heart leap with joy at the presence of God. May your world be orientated around hope, and may you know the strength that comes from knowing that God is for you and not against you.

✦

22nd November May the Holy Spirit bring order in your chaos and create beauty among the ashes. May He bless you with fresh vision and fresh hope every day.

23rd November May you remember God's whisper is louder than evil's roars, and may you have faith to remember that darkness doesn't win; light does.

24th November May the glorious love of the Father dazzle you, the shimmering hope of the Spirit brighten you, and the enfolding love of the Son envelop you.

25th November May the Holy Spirit breathe fresh hope into your soul. May His presence dispel worry, may His peace dissolve trouble, and may truth drive away lies.

26th November Tonight may you remember that the weight does not rest on your shoulders but on God's shoulders. May you know He carries you and that He loves you.

27th November May God's symphony of love cascade over you; may His notes of grace give you hope; may His melody of mercy awaken memories of His image in you.

✦

28th November May the night watches be used by God to mend your emotions, filter your memories, and restore your sense of personhood in Him.

✦

29th November May God give you fresh hope by constantly reminding you that He will finish His work in you, and by lifting your eyes to see into eternity.

30th November May God renew you with restful sleep. May He inspire you with beautiful dreams and awaken you refreshed. May tomorrow overflow with His presence.

December

1st December May Christ's love for you be a lifeline of hope, reminding you that you are loved, freeing you from sin, and anchoring you in the storm.

✦

2nd December May the Father's acceptance give you deep hope that you can face the challenges of tomorrow assured that you will never be alone.

✦

3rd December May God the holy Trinity surround you with hope. The Father has you in His gaze, the Son has you in His prayers, and the Spirit keeps you.

✦

4th December No matter what enemy may try to steal your hope, may you be given grace to cling to the hope that holds you. God's banner over you is love.

5th December In an uncertain world may the certainty of God's promises give you hope. Even death cannot destroy your hope because death is defeated.

✦

6th December May you know the underserved, breathtaking love of God. May His beauty capture your imagination and His kindness melt your heart.

✦

7th December May God's love transform your understanding of yourself and your place in the world; may you be able to see the depth of His love for you.

✦

8th December May you be reminded that nothing can separate you from God's love: no sadness, heartbreak, tragedy, failure, hurt, or enemy.

9th December May you see the love of God in Jesus with new clarity, and may your eyes be lifted from your sins to the cross, where He bore them away for you.

10th December May the Spirit give you a deep assurance of God's love; may any condemnation that grips you be broken; may the failure that stalks you be banished.

11th December May the love of God consume you; may it transform your desires to be in alignment with God's will, birthing a passion for His glory in you.

12th December May your life reflect God's love to others. May they see in you His tenderness; may they encounter His forgiveness and grace through you.

13th December May God give you a joy that is deeper than sorrow; may you find gladness bestowed on you like a garland of blessing and thanksgiving.

14th December May nothing steal your joy. When darkness presses in may God's light cause joy to shimmer, and may joy be deeply rooted in your heart.

15th December May the joy of the Lord be your strength. May you realise that joy is not the same as happiness: it is deep, strong, and persistent.

16th December May your joy flow from the character of God; may your eyes be lifted beyond what you can see to what you cannot see: eternal life.

17th December May you be
given joy in the simple things
of life; may the assurance
that God will never abandon
you lift you from loneliness
forever.

18th December May the struggles you face be overshadowed by the joy that is promised to you as a child of God. May grace hold you in its grip.

✦

19th December May the joy announced by the angels on the night Christ was born be your reality; may faith in Christ be God's gift to you.

✦

20th December May God's peace sustain you in every season of life, giving you unshakeable assurance that winter passes and spring comes again.

✦

21st December May God's peace stand watch over your heart like a sentinel, shielding you from ever feeling alone and reminding you that God wins.

22nd December May God remind you that His peace is not simply the absence of sorrow, but instead it is the gift of His presence always.

✦

23rd December May God give you a deeper revelation of His peace in your life. May nothing steal it from you and may no situation ever overpower you.

✦

24th December May Christ be born in your heart afresh. May His presence drive out fear, His hope drive out despair, and His peace dispel all anxiety.

25th December May the miracle
of the incarnation transform
you; may you know that God
understands your situation and
walks with you through it.

26th December May God's peace bring reconciliation in a troubled world. May the Prince of Peace enable peace in you, your home, and your nation.

27th December May God's grace remind you that He loves you, that He is working in your life, and that He will finish what He has begun.

28th December May you be given grace for the moment and may it be enough; may God remind you that He is with you now, and that this is all the strength you need.

29th December May you be given grace to know that God is always present, always loving, and always good. May He comfort you and sustain you always.

30th December At the end of the year, may God's grace enable you to be honest about your failures, encouraged by your successes, and open to new things.

31st December As you stand on the edge of another year, may God's grace enable you to have confidence, hope, and trust in Him for all that lies ahead.

Photo credits

pp. 14–15 Zach Miles
p. 17 Davide Cantelli
p. 21 Pablo Heimplatz
p. 26 Gaelle Marcel
p. 31 Valeriy Andrushko
pp. 36–37 Martin Brechtl
p. 39 Dan Stark
p. 43 Annie Spratt
p. 48 Aaron Burden
p. 52 Nghia Le
p. 57 Luis Eusebio
p. 62 Billy Pasco
p. 64 Samuel Ferrara
pp. 70–71 Aaron Burden
p. 75 Austin Schmid
p. 76 Eberhard Grossgasteiger
p. 82 Aaron Burden
p. 84 Dino Reichmuth
pp. 86–87 Greg Rakozy
p. 91 Ryoji Iwata
pp. 96–97 Jasper Boer
p. 100 Annie Spratt
p. 102 Ben White
p. 109 Olga Vyshnevska
pp. 112–13 Cmdr Shane
pp. 114–15 Jad Limcaco

p. 117 Jacob Meyer
pp. 122–23 Aaron Burden
p. 125 Hello i m nik
pp. 128–29 Fancy Crave
p. 135 Liane Metzler
p. 136 John Salzarulo
pp. 140–41 Marco Bianchetti
pp. 146–47 Todd Aarnes
p. 153 Frank McKenna
p. 156 Priscilla du Preez
pp. 158–59 John Gibbons

**All images sourced from Unsplash
(https://unsplash.com)**